READING POWER

Sports Training

Basketball

Jack Otten

J 796.323
OTT

The Rosen Publishing Group's
PowerKids Press™
New York

Introduction

Kobe Bryant is a pro basketball player. He plays for the Lakers. The young players below watch the pros play. They want to learn to play basketball better.

Warming Up

The Knights meet for basketball practice. The coach starts practice with a warm-up. The players stretch their arms and legs.

The coach tells the players to run around the court. Running builds strong legs. Strong legs help players to jump high.

Basketball is played on a court.
Each basket is 10 feet high.

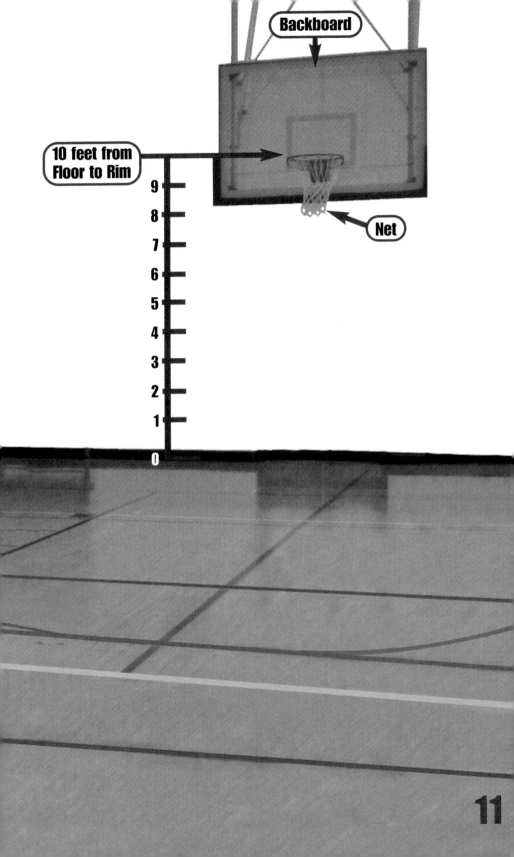

Backboard

10 feet from
Floor to Rim

Net

9
8
7
6
5
4
3
2
1
0

Shooting the Ball

The coach shows the player how to shoot a jump shot. The player holds the ball up to practice his shot. He bends his legs.

The player pushes the ball up and out. He pushes up with his legs, too. He aims for the rim of the basket.

The Knights practice their jump shots. They jump and shoot the ball.

Guarding and Blocking

The coach tells a player how to guard. A player keeps his arms up. Then he reaches out to stop the ball.

The coach tells a player how to block a pass. The player moves to the ball before it reaches the other player. He steals the pass.

Rebounding

The coach tells two players how to rebound a shot. He tells them to look at the rim while another player takes a shot.

The players jump after the ball hits the rim. One player grabs the ball as it comes down. He gets the rebound.

The Knights play a practice game. The team plays the way the coach taught them.

The coach tells the team that they had a good practice. The Knights are learning how to play basketball well.

Glossary

backboard (**bak**-bord) a sheet of glass or wood to which the basket is attached

court (**kort**) an area with painted lines where basketball is played

jump shot (**juhmp shaht**) a basketball shot where the player jumps off the floor and shoots the ball

practice (**prak**-tihs) doing something again and again to learn to do it well

rebound (**ree**-bownd) to grab a basketball shot that has hit off the rim

rim (**rihm**) the edge of the basket to which the net is attached

warm-up (**worm**-uhp) an exercise to get the body ready for work or play

Resources

Books

Basketball in Action
by John Crossingham and Sarah Dann
Crabtree Publishing (2000)

Basketball's Greatest Players
by Sydelle A. Kramer
Random House, Inc. (1997)

Web Site

Basketball Mania
http://tqjunior.thinkquest.org/3952

Index

Word Count: 270

Note to Librarians, Teachers, and Parents

If reading is a challenge, Reading Power is a solution! Reading Power is perfect for readers who want high-interest subject matter at an accessible reading level. These fact-filled, photo-illustrated books are designed for readers who want straightforward vocabulary, engaging topics, and a manageable reading experience. With clear picture/text correspondence, leveled Reading Power books put the reader in charge. Now readers have the power to get the information they want and the skills they need in a user-friendly format.